SEEDS OF THE

Heart

STORMIE CLAY

ISBN 979-8-88616-447-3 (paperback)
ISBN 979-8-88616-448-0 (digital)

Christian Faith Publishing
832 Park Avenue
Meadville, PA 16335
www.christianfaithpublishing.com

Printed in the United States of America

In memory of my godmother Effie Tate. also the meaning of why I chose the name Stormie Clay, While going through the storms of life, God enabled me to endure the tests of time, his handiwork has created and formed me into the woman I am today, look forward to hearing from you soon God Bless.

To all the brothers and sisters who have gone
through loneliness, despair, hopelessness,
only to find out that Jesus Christ has always been there
to mend the broken pieces and give hope to the lost

Thou wilt keep him in perfect peace, whose mind
is stayed on thee, because he trusted in thee.

—Isaiah 26:3 (KJV)

INTRODUCTION

Yes, *God* is real. Real in my soul, for He has washed and made me whole. His love for me is like pure gold. Yes, *God* is real down in my soul.

Dreams and visions are *God's* divine ways of communicating with His people. Being blessed with these gifts can have a profound effect in our daily lives as well as our destiny.

> Before I formed thee in the belly I knew thee;
> and before thou comest forth out of the womb
> I sanctified thee, and I ordained thee a prophet
> unto the nations. (Jeremiah 1:5 KJV)

WHEN DREAMS AND VISIONS BECOME REALITY

As far back as I can remember, at a very young age, I would go to bed and have dreams. I do understand that everybody has dreams. I can only say that most of mine came true. There were times during the night I would have two or three dreams one right after another. Also, there would be times I would be wide awake, and images of people and places would flash like a camera before my natural eyes. Upon awakening, some of the dreams would confuse me. I would go to my mother and ask her for the meaning. Most of the time, her only response and reply was that everybody has dreams. Then I would walk away, feeling dissatisfied. The more I prayed, my understanding of dreams became more clear.

My spiritual journey of dreams began during the year of 1960. I would go to sleep and dream the same dream, standing in front of a white house with a white picket fence, staring at the front door, but I would never open the gate to enter. Once again, as before, I would go to my mother, only to hear the same answer.

I couldn't go to anyone else because my mother was the only person I lived with. I never knew who my dad was nor had I ever met him. My mother never talked about him. Even when I would ask, she just brushed me off.

During the summer of 1967, all the family members were notified to come home to Louisiana. Grandma was sick. The doctor said that she could die soon, so we packed our suitcases and boarded the train from Kansas City, Missouri, to Grandma's house.

By 6:00 p.m. that Friday, all of the family members had arrived at my grandma's five-bedroom house. It was now occupied with six adults and about twenty children screaming and running around everywhere. Two of my favorite aunties decided to go to the store to pick up some food for dinner. I was surprised that they only asked me to go with them and didn't ask any of the other children to go. I really felt good about it, being next to the oldest child there.

After all the shopping, we got into the car. One thing I thought was strange is that we were not going down the same street that we had taken to get to the store. Out of curiosity, I asked one of my aunts, "Where are we going?"

Her reply, "Don't worry about it. We're going to visit a close friend of ours."

My eyes nearly popped out of my head. There, at that very moment, the car stopped right in front of a white house with a picket fence. Both of my aunts got out of the car. "Come on and get out, Naomi. We just want you to meet your real dad for the first time."

Right then, flashbacks of all the dreams I had about a white house truly had become a reality. At that very moment, I started walking through the gate.

The Vietnam war had already begun. A classmate of mine, one of her brothers got drafted at the age of nineteen. He had been sched-uled to be shipped out that Sunday, headed to California for basic training. That Friday, his sister invited me to a going away party. I went but deep within, I felt very sad. All I could hear was an inner voice saying, *He's never coming back.*

Even though everybody was happy, some were eating, some dancing, others were drinking, I just couldn't get into the mood, and the weirdest thing is the whole time, the way that I was feeling and the voice that I kept on hearing, I couldn't even tell his family. It was like I wanted to say something, but I couldn't open my mouth to say anything. In a way, I felt guilty.

He left Kansas City on an airplane early Sunday morning, so I was told by his sister. Early Monday morning, instead of getting ready to go school, I began crying. Tears just flowed down my face. I couldn't stop. My mother came into the bedroom and asked me what

　　　　　　　　STORMIE CLAY

was wrong, if I were sick. All I could do was shake my head and say, "No, Mama, something bad is about to happen."

She replied, "What is going to happen?"

"I can't say, Mama, I can't say."

From that Monday to Saturday, day and night, I cried, didn't eat, or drink. I awoke each morning crying and went to bed crying.

On Thursday, Mother came into my bedroom and said that if I was still crying, she was going to take me to the doctor and have me sent to a mental hospital.

That Saturday night, I went to sleep and dreamt I was on a battlefield with all kinds of ammunition flying over my head, flames of fire were all around me, I saw men everywhere, running and hiding, trying to avoid getting hurt. Then all of a sudden, I heard an explosion, like a bomb, light and fire so bright. I then jumped up out of bed and ran through the house to the front door. The light was so bright I even ran out the front door to see where the noise came from and looked toward the east in the back of our house because in the past, airplanes had been known to crash in the Fairfax district near the airport.

I came back into the house and looked at the clock on the living room wall, and it was three o'clock in the morning. I went back into the bedroom.

Sunday, I stopped crying around seven o'clock. I heard a woman screaming and hollering, knocking on the front door of our house. Mama said, "Hurry up and open the door. See who that is this time of the morning. Sounds like they're hurt."

When I opened the door, my friend's grandmother nearly fell to the floor on her face. She had a Western Union letter in her hand. She could barely speak. My mother took the letter and read it out loud. It stated that the grandson, while he was in Vietnam, had stepped on a land mine and was blown all to pieces. Then my mother started crying too.

The army shipped his body back to the States. It was then transferred to Louisiana to be laid to rest. My friend came over and invited me to go with the family to the funeral. I refused to go. I told her that I had already mourned all week. I kissed her and gave her a hug.

The family brought pictures of him. The casket was bronze with a piece of glass at the top. I could see his head. The family said that his head was the only part of his body they could find and put in the casket. The rest was in pieces. The military army serviceman gave his mother a United States flag and a ten-thousand-dollar check. What good did all that mean when you had lost a son to a war he didn't understand? Most of all, sadly, his life was cut so short.

June 1, 1993. I awoke early that Monday morning and sat on the side of the bed. Like a camera, I saw a cemetery and three black funeral cars. I took both of my hands and wiped my face, yet I still saw the same visions going on now for about three weeks. I smelled the scent of flowers and didn't have even one plant in my home because my cat would chew on them and make itself sick. I heard the sound of an organ playing two gospel hymns: "What a Friend We Have in Jesus" and "Nobody's Fault but Mine."

Monday, July 1, 1993. I was awoken that morning with cold chills all over my body. Feeling sad, I called my children and told them to pray and told them that someone in the family was going to die, but at that present moment, I couldn't say who. All that day, I couldn't do any housework. All I could do was pray and ask the Lord who He was about to take from our family. I lay down on the couch in my living room, still restless. I fell asleep.

Around four-thirty, a knock on the door. It was one of my younger sisters. As I sat straight up on the couch to look at her, I could not see her face. I could see like a shadow of her from her head to her feet, but I could not see her face. I wiped my eyes, thinking I could have a better sight, and yet, there stood my sister right in front of me. We talked about cooking and getting together at the lake for the Fourth of July, then she left and said that she would see me later.

That Thursday, at 11:00 p.m., I received a phone call from my nephew saying that my sister and her boyfriend had been shot and that the both of them were dead. At that very moment, all I could do was take a deep breath, pick up the phone, and call the police department and tell them what had happened.

I arrived at my sister's house in about thirty minutes, only to stand outside the door and see the ambulance attendant bring her

   STORMIE CLAY

body out of the house on a stretcher, her whole body covered up with a sheet. As they lifted up the stretcher, I lifted up the sheet covered all in blood. I could not see my sister's face.

After reaching the hospital, on the trauma unit, doctors reported she had been shot at close range with a .45 Magnum revolver in her face. The boyfriend died immediately by a self-inflicted gunshot wound to the head.

I have had many dreams, but one in particular that stays on my mind involved my sister's death in 1993. I lay down in bed that night, the day before her funeral, closed my eyes, and when I opened them, there I was, standing in an unknown place with darkness all around. There, with open pits in the ground, out of them came huge flames of fire and smoke. There were people trying to crawl out of these pits of flames. The more they tried to crawl out, they fell back in. They were crying, some moaning. They had no eye sockets; they were empty holes. All around, there were charred building remains. "Oh what a terrible place!" I said to myself.

I looked right to left, and as I turned to look, straight in front of me, there stood my sister. I looked down at my feet. There I was, standing atop of three white stairs, my sister at the bottom. She had no body. It was all black. I could see only her head, not her feet. Both of her hands were cupped together. In them, she held a white candle, but it wasn't lit. She said, "I don't want to be here. The other people don't want to be here either."

I said to her, "I don't want to be here, not in this place."

I awoke at that very moment. I asked the Lord God where He took me. I heard the word *Sheol*. I repeated the word *Sheol*, then I reached for my Bible dictionary and looked up the definition. In some scriptures, it means hades or hell, a place of torment for the wicked. All I could say was, "Oh my *God*, is that where my sister went?" But I can truly say six months before her death, she rejected God and made a horrible statement that God had never done anything for her. While riding back home in her car, I prayed that the good Lord would not strike the car with a bolt of lightning.

Early one Saturday, in the month of April 2010, I decided to go fishing, one of my favorite pastimes. So I packed up my fishing equipment, invited one of my younger daughters to go with me, and we headed down Highway 70 West to a lake where a coworker said he had gone and caught plenty of fish. While driving, I had this horrible feeling come over me, so I just started praying. All of a sudden, about midway of the journey, I turned the car around in the middle of the street and headed back toward home. At that very instant, like a camera, I had a vision of my mother lying in a casket.

My daughter asked, "Mama, what's wrong? We came all this way to go fishing, and now we're going back home."

My reply was, "I can't talk right now but later."

At that present time, my mother had just turned eighty-six years old and was living in a nursing home. For several days, I was restless. I had made plans to go and visit her. I had even told my daughter I was going to visit her, then on a Thursday morning, I heard a still voice say, *Go and visit your mother because she is going to die, and tell her that you have forgiven her.* So I got in a hurry and went to see my mother for the last time.

On July 4, during a family reunion celebration, the nursing home contacted a family member and said my mother had passed away at three o'clock in the morning. Deep in my heart, I was so glad that I had been obedient to what I know now spiritually as the Holy Spirit and that He had told me what to do. As the years come and go, I thank *God* for the gift. For it is hard for even my children to surprise me, for every time I have a dream about going fishing, somebody is usually pregnant.

STORMIE CLAY

WHAT IS LIFE?

To some of us, life may be just living in this world from day to day,
being able to get up every morning, going about each his own way.
Never stopping to think who gave us life, enabling us to do the things
    we do.
God is the only one, He made me and you.
Man cannot give the necessities of today,
only *God* can give it to us, only He can take it away.
Life's not worth living, when *God's* not in your heart.
To know Him and love Him, life's a brand-new start.
What does your life mean not knowing who you really are?
If *God's* not within you, life can't go too far.
Life can be very pleasant, as happy as can be.
For when you know the Word of *God*, His truth can make you free.

(April 12, 1974)

WHY GOD CREATED GRANDMOTHERS

What Mama can't do, Grandma can
What Mama don't tolerate, Grandma can stand
What Mama don't cook, Grandma has already done
When Mama seems strict, with Grandma you have fun
When Mama is angry, Grandma, she smiles
Grandma will spoil you, make you a rotten child
When Mama tells you no, with Grandma, it's all right
Just don't tell Mama you stayed up late on a school night
Grandma will tuck you in bed, tell you stories of old
Things your Mama got away with when she was a little girl
I know why *God* created grandmothers, you see
For I am one of those Grandmas, I myself and me.

(January 15, 1999)

HELP

Hear me heavenly Father, please answer my prayer
High above the heavens, I know You are there
Grant me peace and serenity
Help me to know grace and dignity
Forgive me, Lord, for being out of hand
To speak those things, which I should understand
Wipe away my secret tears, give me boldness instead of fear
Guide me through this forsaken land, lift me up, hold my hands
And when I should question You again, have mercy on me, an igno-
    rant woman in sin.

(June 3, 2017)

TROUBLED

Why am I screaming when no one hears
Why do I cry when no one sees my tears
When I am in pain, nobody feels my anguish
I leap for joy, no one knows that I'm happy
When my heart feels sorrow, who will share my sympathy
Though I'm angry, who cares whether I'm mad
My mind desires peace, my enemies are at war
Yet why am I still screaming even more than before
I wander around in darkness, blinded by the light, I'm so confused
I don't have the strength to continue the fight
If I give up, my soul will be damned, sin has taken full control
I'll just keep on screaming, in hopes that someone will hear
To enlighten my heart, take away the fear.

(July 7, 2005)

WHEN I PRAY

When I pray, I pray for all family, friends, both great and small
The world and those who live therein, those who are saved, those
    still in sin
Neighbors, enemies, I know not all their names
When I pray, it's all the same
Night after night, day by day, I would not know, if I didn't pray
I couldn't love or be kind, if I didn't pray, I would lose my mind
Over and over my constant words, I pray,
"Dear Lord, I hope that You heard
Sometimes I feel a little distressed, Lord, for me, is this a test"
After all is said and done, I rise from my knees, victory is won
When life is over, my soul set free, now I wonder, "Lord, who on this
    earth has prayed for me?"

(September 28, 2006)

WHEN GOD KEEPS ME

When God keeps me, I have no worries or fear
For in my quiet moments, He is near
Constantly speaking to my heart, penetrating every inch part by part
When God keeps me, I dare not cry, for He knows when I truly try
To be the best that I can, He knows what I can stand
Though my trials sometimes seem hard, I am lost, I think about
    Jesus, who died on the cross
I can do all things through Christ, who strengthens me,
When God keeps me, I am totally free

(January 15, 1999)

WAITING ON THE LORD

I know patience in the Lord, I do wait
I feel love instead of hate
I know long-suffering, it brings hope, especially with others,
I've learned to cope
I've mastered peace, joy to gain, Jesus's words, what sweet refrain
Through charity, no riches or gold, through forgiveness, self-control
Temperance has sheltered all of me, I once was blinded, now I see
With His hands, a tender touch, He loves me so very much
To those that are going where I have been, away from strife, away
    from sin
I know Jesus, for He is real in my daily life,
I no longer struggle through all the pain and strife

(August 3, 1994)

GOD'S MERCY

I would have not known mercy if it had not been for the Lord,
Daily I meditate in His Word,
Trusting in Him as I journey through
Joy and pain, totally free, a crown of life to gain.
Though the paths seem difficult, each time I began to fall,
Trials of life forsake, I have found a friend, an outstretched hand,
Without the Lord, I shall not stand,
Dear Lord, accept me for who I am,
For You will do what no man can, change my mind,
Renew the person in me, shape, mold, unfold, set my soul free.

(June 25, 1994)

NOBODY BUT JESUS

Who can change the course of this world, the moon, stars, nature itself,
Nobody but Jesus
Provides the air in the atmosphere we breathe,
Man, animals, the leaves on the trees
Changes the hearts of any woman or man, already has created the
    master plan,
Nobody but Jesus
Changes the clouds formed in the sky,
The seasons winter, summer, spring, and fall,
The power of His wisdom, every drop of rain, the entire earth declares
    His majesty,
Can reverse the hands of time, whose name the angels in heaven
    proclaim.
Who can we turn to in times of despair and need,
Who can help determine our actions to succeed, nobody but Jesus.

(April 11, 2016)

NO PEACE

Got up this morning with trouble on my mind,
no one to turn to, no peace to find,
my home in shambles, children gone astray,
Friends don't have time to listen, who cares anyway.
Hurt and confused, my life's gone downhill, mind spinning around,
How can I look up, when my head is bowed down,
many voices began to speak to me,
end your life, let your soul be free,
turning to the streets, nothing was there,
all confused, going nowhere,
the bottle will not cure me, money can't buy,
nothing seems to work, many times I try,
there's a peace I need within me from on high,
save me, dear Lord, don't let my soul die.

(July 30, 2003)

TIMES OF DESPAIR

Clouds of darkness hang over me,
Lord, where can I go, when shall I be free?
Going through trials and tribulations downtrodden,
I have been misused and brokenhearted.
The stairways of life, ups and downs,
no peace, no love, nowhere to be found.
Confusion deeply embedded within my head,
my spirit is lifeless, my body is dead.
Hopes and dreams all shattered and torn,
tears continue to fall, all I do is sit and mourn.
Lord, I need Your help, please make me strong,
help me to stand upright, correct the wrong.

(May 26, 2005)

JESUS'S LOVE

There's no sweeter love that man can claim, than to share it with
    another in Jesus's name.
A love that shall never end, knowing Jesus is forever a friend
Who knows the secrets of the heart, a love no man can tear apart,
Built on the promises, everlasting life, bought with a price, suffering
    and strife
Held between the heavenly Father's hand, holy words only given to man,
Love will always be the key, an open door to make men free.

(December 28, 1990)

ODE TO A LADY

While reading the newspaper on today, I glanced at an article that
        read to say,
Jackie Onassis Kennedy has died, also where her body should lie.
Only memories of the dreaded past, of a woman's courage through
        years had last,
worn eyes of tears, yet a face of pride, a tower of strength at her side,
        I wondered so many times how this could be, you were stronger
        than any ship tossed at sea.
Through sorrow and life's constant lost, for you have truly paid the cost,
a mother and friend to all, Jackie, you knew your innermost call
a leader serene and true, showing a nation what to do.
Dignity, personality, a loving smile, you too were a mother's child
Jackie you may not know, but you'll be sadly missed, you have given
        splendid bliss,
the clothes you wore, the way you walked, a gentle voice when you
        talked,
it didn't matter, the color of skin, Jackie, we understand where you
        have been,
only a special person like you could stand, touching heart to hearts,
        from hand to hand
Jackie, you have done your job, did your best, the battle is over, you
        have conquered the test,
never to be forgotten, mind and soul free, Jackie, you were better
        than any soldier could ever be.

(June 25, 1994)

BINDING LOVE

To know love is to give love, when all else fails, just like when a ship
    needs a sail.
Love has no enemies, only friends, love is everlasting unto the end
Hope and trust in what we feel, love isn't fake it should be real
Welcome the arms of another, love will always be together.
Why blame others when in fault for mischievous deeds will be caught
Treat everyone in ways we want to feel, some things in life haven't
    been real,
share each other's little mistakes, understanding that's all it takes,
so go ahead, take someone by the hand, give them a boost, a helping
    hand.
For you will never know who's in need, do yourself a favor, do a good
    deed.

(November 12, 1991)

WITHOUT GOD'S GRACE

What if God slumbered or slept? Worlds would collide, saints not
be kept.
The sun would not shine nor clouds give rain, man not exist, more
suffering, more pain
Hope and peace, a thing of the past, the prayers of the righteous
would not last
Hatred ever abounding, love decreased, more sinful deeds, killing
increased,
Yes, what if God slumbered and slept? His eyes never opened, tears
never wept?
Without His love, mercy, and grace, this entire world a horrible place.

(July 5, 1994)

REMEMBERING DADDY

I knelt down to pray today, not expecting to be very long for I was in
a hurry, my daddy will be coming home,
I opened my eyes to see him standing near, my heart was racing, his
voice I long to hear.
I listened for an open door, footsteps soft yet strong, hurry up, Daddy,
you're really taking too long,
his hands would feel so gentle as he placed them upon my head, how
I would feel so peaceful, nothing to dread.
The smile he had on his face when he came into my bedroom, I just
kept on praying, oh, Lord, let my daddy come home real soon.
Time was passing, it was getting very late, I wanted to be ready, for
I had a hot date,
as I turned around to see, it was my mother standing in my room,
she told me my daddy was gone, he will not be coming home.
She said he whispered that he loved me, not to worry, keep a smile on
my face, for he had to leave me to go to a better place.
His time had come, the Lord he had to meet, for he had another
family waiting a very special seat.
So now when I say my prayers, I can truly stand, for there will never be
another daddy like mine in my life, for, Daddy, you were the man.

(July 1, 2009)

SOMETIMES IT'S GOOD TO CRY

Overwhelmed by the trials of life today, I come to a place of solitude
     hidden away,
trying not to worry, why should I care, with hopes of being loved
     sometimes, somehow, somewhere
I never knew my daddy, Mama is all I had, no dreams come true,
     deep within I'm sad.
Sometimes it's good to cry.
Nobody really knows me, I barely know myself, oh please, can some-
     one listen, I'm calling out for help.
In the middle of the night, my mind began to roam, I'm out here,
     believe me, I wanna go home,
don't want to lose anything, got to have control, sometimes it's hard
     to focus when life has treated you cold,
sometimes it's good to cry.
All filled up with life's pressures and pain, only to start another day
     all over again,
I had a talk with Jesus, He's now my special friend, He says He really
     loves me until the very end,
I don't have to worry or fear, because I know He's always near,
So now when life's troubles slowly pass me by,
It's good to know Jesus when I begin to cry.

(May 4, 1999)

GUIDANCE

Lord, teach me what I should know,
Guide my paths where to go,
Uphold me with Your tender hand, forever keep Your holy plan,
I'm just a woman, yet don't fully understand, just show me I know
I can
With Your help, be strong and good, close out this world, live by
Your Word.
Please, Lord, don't let me fall, hear my prayers, hear my call,
In the midnight hours when there's unrest, comfort my soul so I can
be blessed
Make me, Lord, to cherish Your tender love, give me peace from
heaven above.

(June 29, 2008)

THANK YOU

Thank You, Jesus, for this day, for keeping me safe along the way.

Though my days are filled with stress, through Your Word, I'm truly
blessed

Trials and tribulations surely come, I call on You, Lord Jesus, the
Holy One

Sometimes it's difficult, I can barely stand, I constantly reach for
Your outstretched hand

Who will listen, help me to understand, You're all that I know, You
have the plan

To mold me into the godly woman You would have me to be, oh,
dear Jesus, my source, my key

To open closed doors, shut by man's hands, I'm waiting on You, Jesus,
You are the one who will understand.

(November 8, 2015)

REMEMBER ME

I hope that when I die, I'll come back and see
Just how I looked and hear what people will say about me
Will I be dressed in an old dress or new frock
In a brown casket or a pink paper box
Words truly spoken good or bad
Will my heart feel sorry or be made glad
Will songs be sung of my life's story tell, or just stared upon,
forgotten like a bottomless well
Relatives and friends, will they cry, will I be missed or just another
goodbye
Oh yes, one thing I almost forgot, before I'm dumped in a hole then
covered with dirt or rocks
Now my soul, where shall I fly free, back to *God* because He'll
remember me.

(July 7, 1994)

BOUND BY WITCHCRAFT

Introduction

In today's society, we as a people can openly discuss topics from politics, wars, religion, abortion, racism, same-sex marriages. Why not witchcraft? There are hundreds of people around the world today that may have had some experiences or have communicated with friends or family members who have practiced some form of witchcraft or devil worship. There are many people who have had spells cast on them by some wicked person, not knowing what has actually happened to them without explanation why their mind has become confused, out-of-control behavior, only to be locked away in a room in a mental ward, medicated with all types of antipsychotic drugs.

The question: is there a cure? Medically, what does a person or family do when confronted with this situation? Do they pick up the telephone? Or in today's modern world, text 911 witch doctor? Well, for those of us who do not believe or are trying to avoid the subject, this practice and belief can be traced as far back into the biblical days of Jesus, passed down from generation to generation of witches and warlocks. Right now, somewhere in our neighborhoods, behind closed doors, there are people, even loved ones, who have sold their souls to the devil.

The following information are eyewitness accounts that I have not only seen with my own eyes, but on numerous occasions, I was invited to be in the presence of those that were affected by the sin-sick mind of others.

Out of respect and to protect and most of all, the love and guidance of the Holy Spirit, the names of individuals involved have been withheld. Some are now deceased and others yet live on right today. Praise the Lord for those like me who have accepted Jesus Christ as their personal Savior and overcame Satan's power.

> For no weapon form against a child of *God* shall
> prosper. (Isaiah 54:17 KJV)

Manasseh reigned as the thirteenth king of Judah over Jerusalem,

> and he caused his children to pass through the fire in the valley of the son of Hinnom, also he observed times, and used enchantments, and used witchcraft, and dealt with a familiar spirit, and with wizards, he wrought much evil in the sight of the Lord, to provoke him to anger. (2 Chronicles 33:6 KJV)

1

In the spring of 1957, my mother received a long-distance telephone call from relatives in Louisiana that she should come down there as soon as possible, that one of her great-aunties was at the point of death. The doctors had given up. There was nothing else that they could do for her. Mother packed only one suitcase. Off to the train station we went. We had traveled to Louisiana many times before, but for some reason, this journey was not going to be the same. Even though I was only seven years old, I was having some strange feelings. I could not quite understand or explain. Little did I know I was about to find out.

The train arrived at 3:00 p.m., downtown Shreveport, Louisiana. We were met by a great-uncle who led us out to the parking lot to get into his car. While sitting in the back seat, I heard him say to my mother that her aunt had stated that she was not going to die until she saw my mother's face.

     STORMIE CLAY

We arrived in front of an old three-story brick building. We then got out and walked up a long flight of stairs until we got to the third floor. My great-uncle knocked on the door. As the door slowly opened, we walked in, and sitting in the front room of my auntie's apartment were many other relatives. They all came around and hugged and kissed my mother and me. Both sides of my cheeks were red and sore.

As we walked toward Auntie's bedroom, another relative opened the door. She had tears in her eyes. There lay Auntie in bed, with her head turned facing the window. When she heard my mother call her name, she turned her head to see who was speaking to her. She slightly smiled and, barely speaking, she said, "Oh my dear niece, I am so happy to see you. Is that your little girl?"

My mother nodded her head and said, "Yes."

She asked me to come close to the bed so she could see me. She then reached for my hand. Then she asked for a drink of Coca-Cola. My mother picked up the bottle, placed it to her lips, and she took a small sip, took one deep breath, her head fell back on the pillow, and she was gone. My mother screamed out, "She's gone, she's gone!"

I was pushed to the side as the bedroom door came open. While everyone was standing around the bed, crying, I noticed that Auntie's mouth was wide open. I had never seen a person die before, but right there, before my very eyes, a grey mist came out of her mouth, encircled her head, and wiggled like a snake. Then it went out the bedroom window.

The doctor was called to come and pronounce her dead. When he arrived, family members asked the doctor to perform an autopsy. They were all curious about her death. How could Auntie have been so healthy and all of a sudden die?

A week later, the results from the autopsy came back. Cause of death: unknown. Family members were not satisfied. I overheard them talking when I should have been asleep like the other children. One of the other aunties said that the doctor said that when they opened up Auntie's stomach, the coroner pulled out a snake about six inches long. I heard one of the family members mention the word *hoodoo*, something I had never heard of before. Also the word *two-*

headed people. I then became very afraid. In my mind, I though, *Are there monsters in the state of Louisiana?*

The next day, my mother left with some of the family members. They were gone so long I couldn't count the hours. All I know is the sun was going down.

After the funeral, my mother and I were taken back to the train station, and we traveled back to Kansas City. We were met by my daddy.

Later on that evening, while sitting at the dinner table, my daddy asked, "How was the trip?"

And my mother told him all the details about the death, the autopsy, most of all, about the two-headed person. She went on to explain how that Auntie didn't die of natural causes, that a woman that she had befriended thought she was dating her husband, and she brought Auntie a plate of food. Unknowingly, she had put snake eggs in it, and Auntie ate the food. Mother went on to say that the snake had been inside so long that it had grown and attached itself to her intestines. Oh yes, I found out that a two-headed person was someone who could tell fortunes and also practiced hoodoo.

2

July, summer of 1962, I was sitting on the front porch of our house when a green four-door Chevy pulled up. All of a sudden, out jumped Reverend GQ. He would always come over to our house every Sunday. But today, being a Thursday, something had to be very important. As he walked upon the porch, I could smell an odor like dead fish. Even though he was dressed in his brown suit, I said, "Oh *God*, he had gotten up this morning and didn't take a bath."

"Where's your mother?" he asked. "Go and tell her to come here quickly."

I ran inside the house. Mama came rushing out the door. When she saw the reverend, she asked him, "What's wrong?"

He grabbed a chair and sat down and pulled off both of his shoes. There on his feet were maggots crawling in and out the holes. Some even fell out onto the floor. He told Mama that on awakening that morning, when he pulled back the covers on his bed, that's when he saw the numerous holes. Maggots everywhere. Mama asked what happened. His reply was, "Sister, I don't really know."

Once again, I heard Mama speak of a two-headed person who lived in the state of Missouri, and he could help him. But he would have to drive over to this person's house. Being twelve years old now, Mama said I could go with them, that it would be a learning experience for me.

So off the old green Chevy sped across the freeway until we drove up in front of an old redbrick building. Again, we walked up a long flight of stairs until we came to an apartment door, the numbers 636. Mama knocked three times. A small-framed little woman answered the door. Mama asked for the doctor. We slowly walked into a big black painted room with lit candles everywhere, all different colors—red, black, white, and purple. There was also the smell of incense all over the entire apartment. This was no doctor's office I had ever visited before, at least not for a checkup.

I wasn't allowed to enter the dining room, but I sat in the living room. Soon a dark-skinned man, medium build, dressed in a long black robe with his head covered with a turban entered the room. Mama introduced the reverend to Dr. Casey. Before the reverend could open his mouth, he was asked to sit down at the dining room table.

He began telling the reverend that he had been dating two different women at the same time. One of them found out about the other, had stolen a set of keys to his apartment, took a pair of his shoes, and took them to a witchcraft person, and they dressed them. The Cajun two-headed man told the reverend that he could help him, but he would have to pay a fee. The reverend agreed. That's when Dr. Casey got up from the table, went into another room, and brought out a blue glass bottle, set it on the table, and told the reverend what to do. Also, he gave him a piece of paper, told him to recite the words for seven days, and anoint his feet with the solution that was in the bottle. The reverend thanked the man and reached into his back pocket, pulled out his billfold, took out some green dollar bills, and handed them to him.

We then left the apartment building, back to the car, headed back to Kansas City, Kansas, back to our house. The reverend thanked Mama and drove off.

Seven days passed by. On the eighth day, the reverend came back to our house. Only this time, when he got out of his car, he had a big smile on his face. "Hurry up and go get your mama. I have got to show her my feet."

When Mama came out on the porch, the reverend had taken off both of his shoes. "Sister, it worked, it worked," he said. "Look at my feet."

When I stared down at his feet, they were as smooth as a baby's skin. No more holes, no more maggots, and thank God, the foul smell was gone. That's when the reverend pulled out his billfold once again, took out some dollar bills, and handed them to Mama. She had a great big smile on her face. She just folded the bills and placed them inside her bra. She never said how much it was. All I know is that we had a good dinner that night.

Summer of 1969, a very close friend of mine became seriously ill. Her mother and mine were close friends as well. One day, I overheard their conversation in the kitchen at our house, that my friend had awaken about two weeks ago screaming and hollering, complaining about a headache, that she could hear strangers' voices talking to her. She would lock herself in the bathroom, and it would be difficult to get her to come out, her hair was falling out in large patches, and her monthly period had stopped about three months ago.

After hearing all the terrible things that my friend was going through, I became very upset. How could this have happened to such a nice person? Oh *God*, my friend was only nineteen years old at the time with a good future ahead of her. Her mother had taken her to several doctors to no avail.

My friend ended up being admitted to a nearby hospital in a psychiatric unit for a couple of weeks, only to be discharged back home in the same condition. Finally, her mother called my mother and said she was about to pack up and take my friend to Arkansas, that someone she had met told her that a family member of theirs had that same problem, and they had taken them to see a two-headed hoodoo person that could break spells off of people.

That next day, my friend was gone on a journey that I prayed she would return normal again. That one day turned into years. I never heard of what actually happened. All I know is that her mother contacted mine and said that my friend was living in another state.

Summer of 1985, I was visiting my godmother's home. I would always go by and check on her to see if she needed me to run around and do some errands. She was an authentic church gossiper. She had been a member of a local Baptist church for over twenty years. No doubt, she knew just about everything and everybody. Usually on some days, I'm in a hurry, grab the money, and run. But Godmother asked me to sit down in her recliner because she had something very important to tell me about what happened to the whore of Babylon, one of the flirty women that also attended the same church.

This is her side of the story. She said that the woman always sat next to her in church on the same row every Sunday. She seemed to have been a nice person, a little free-spirited toward the men in church, kind of dressed very provocatively. Although Godmother said there were others as well, it had been rumored that the woman was having an affair with one of the husbands of the mothers in church.

So last Sunday, the mother walked over to the woman and handed her a five-dollar bill. The woman smiled at the mother, took the five-dollar bill, and thanked her. Godmother said that the woman didn't put the money in the offering plate when it was passed around but opened up her purse and put it in there. She said that for the last three Sundays, the woman had not been attending church. But the pastor stood up in church and made an announcement that the woman was sick. So he was asking for volunteers to go with him to the woman's house and pray for her.

Good old Godmother, she agreed to be one of the volunteers. Everyone met with the pastor after church to meet at the woman's home at 3:00 p.m. Godmother said that on entering the house, they were taken to the bedroom, and when the door was opened, there lay the woman in bed, her eyes were open, but she could not speak.

She just nodded her head. Her whole body was covered with a white sheet up to her neck. Only her head was visible.

The whole group gathered around the bed to pray. The pastor asked the woman for her hand to join in prayer. At that very moment, when she raised up her hand, the sheet fell off, and Godmother said that both of her hands had large boils all over them, purple, like big clusters of grapes. You could barely see her fingers. After prayer, everyone left.

Three days later, the pastor once again stood up in church and announced that the woman had passed away. Godmother said that while sitting at a church dinner, she overheard that the church mother believed in witchcraft and had gotten her revenge.

These are only a few of the incidents that I encountered by association with other people. To write all of it would take more than just a few pieces of paper.

OVERCOMING WITCHCRAFT THROUGH JESUS CHRIST

Introduction

The story that you are about to read has been written in chronological order. These are true accounts witnessed and experienced by myself, which took place in my hometown of Kansas. Those who read this may not understand or may have had the same similar incidents happen to them or a family member or a close friend. I have also learned down through the years that when trying to run away from the evils in life, sometimes a person can run right into the same situation all over again, only to find themselves surrounded by wickedness. It is better to run to *God*. It doesn't matter whether it be family or friends. It is a good thing to be walking in the light of *God*'s Word than to be stumbling around in darkness.

Some of these statements written in this book may seem a bit too graphic, but it is the truth, the whole truth, nothing but the truth. These satanic incidents happened to me, and I will never forget them.

> Now the works of the flesh are manifest which are these; Adultery, Fornication, Uncleanness, Lasciviousness, Idolatry, Witchcraft, Sorcery, Hatred, Variance, Emulations, Wrath, Strife, Seditions, Heresies, Envyings, Murders, Drunkenness, Revellings, and such like of the which I tell you before, as I have told you in the past, that

they which do such things shall not inherit the
kingdom of *God*. (Galatians 5:19–21 KJV)

This story is dedicated to my children, all eight of them, in hopes and many prayers that have gone up before the Lord God. Not only would they learn from me how to depend upon Jesus, the Word (Holy Bible), but to be aware of their surroundings, to be careful. Spiritual discernment is the key. And to those who will listen and take heed, may the Lord forever bless and keep them, sheltered under His mighty wings of protection.

"Behold I send you forth as sheep in the midst of wolves, Be ye therefore wise as serpents, and harmless as doves" (Matthew 10:16 KJV).

1

It was the summer of 1963, the weather hot and humid. School was out. No more hassles and headaches of doing homework. I had just turned thirteen years old. It was at that very time in my life I experienced my first encounter with voodoo/hoodoo, witchcraft, black magic, or whatever a person may want to call it.

I had just finished playing a game of kickball with some of the neighborhood children when I felt something warm and sticky run down my legs between my thighs. Off to the bathroom I ran, and to my surprise, I noticed there was blood all over my panties. *Oh God. I am dying. I am never going to be the same. My whole life ruined.*

No matter what stories that a person may hear or be told, substitute names, you may want to call your period the curse, riding the white horse. It is still a natural part of growing up and becoming a woman every young girl goes through. I was so embarrassed that I didn't tell my mother until about two days later. All I know is that she was complaining about the toilet paper going so fast. I finally confessed that I was the culprit. She just handed me a package of sanitary napkins and reminded me to stop using all of the toilet paper in the house.

From that day on, as my menstrual cycle came around each month, I felt so insecure wearing those thick white cotton pads

     STORMIE CLAY

between my thighs. It made my panties bulge out so much my private area appeared to have swollen up three times its normal size. To tell the whole truth, I stopped wearing pants. I started wearing only dresses so that when I sat down in a chair, it wouldn't look as if I had grown a pair of balls.

2

As time went by, I became more adjusted to the mere fact I was in the process of becoming a woman. I thought that whatever happens now to my body at this point would be very personal, and I didn't want anyone else to know about it. So, privately, I began to separate my soiled underwear from the other laundry. I would put them in a plastic bag, place the bag as far back into the corner of the bathroom cabinet as possible so no one could see them.

Every Friday was laundry day, and I went to the bathroom to get my underwear. I reached into the cabinet, and as far as I placed my hand, there was no plastic bag to be found. I knew where I put them. I searched every cabinet possible, yet no plastic bag. I was at that point of frustration. I then went to my mother and told her what was going on. Her response was that she had found the bag, opened it, and saw the soiled underwear. She then took all four pairs out of the bag, only to find that the crotch had been cut out of them. It looked as if someone had taken a pair of scissors and purposely cut just around the bloodstained area of all four pairs of my panties.

My eyes nearly popped out of my head. My thoughts ran rampant. Who could have done such a terrible thing? Invaded my privacy? It was very degrading as well as nasty. I wanted this person punished. All my mother could say was, "Don't worry." But how could I not worry?

Three days later, I overheard an unusual conversation that my mother was having over the telephone with one of her friends. She said that while we were away from the house, someone had broken into our house, found my bag of underwear, and did witchcraft on them. Oh my *God*, there I was, too young to do anything about it. I had never heard anyone talk such a mess before.

That night, before I went to bed, I got down on my knees and prayed to *God* Almighty to help me. *Why, God, would anyone just take my underwear when there were two other women in the household that were also having periods?*

Each day became more difficult for me to bear. My nerves were shattered. I could not eat and barely fell asleep. I tried to pray and read my Bible. Each night, my pillows were soaked with tears of despair. *Why, God? Have I been such a terrible person? A thirteen-year-old child who tried to be obedient to my mother, the only parent in my life, how could this bad situation that I am going through affect me? God, do you love me? Are you even listening?*

One night, while I was lying in bed, trying to go to sleep, I felt like I had the urgency to go to the bathroom to pee. The very moment I stood up, my private area felt actually weird as if someone was taking their fingers and opening me up, and to my surprise, as I pulled down my panties, there was a big black beetle about the size of a silver dollar. It fell off my crotch, down onto the floor, and ran underneath the bed.

I immediately fell to the floor on my knees to see which direction it went. Like into thin air, it disappeared; like a ghost, it was gone. All of a sudden, I fainted, lights out. I don't remember how long I was out.

I woke up to find myself on the floor between the bed and the bathroom. My mind went into overdrive shock. What if there were more of these insects crawling around inside my body? How could I get them all out? *Should I just go in to the bathroom and drink some concoction of medicine to make me throw up without killing myself, damning my soul to hell? Or maybe take a clothes hanger and push it up into my private area as far as it will go, then bleed to death before anyone would find me? Oh God, I need your help. Please don't let me lose my mind.*

I did not say anything to anyone, not even my mother. There was no one to help me anyway. I did not want to end up in the hospital in the mental ward. I just prayed even harder, hoping deep within my heart, one day, I would get an answer. Things couldn't have gotten any worse.

Months went by. My private area didn't open up anymore nor did anything else crawl out.

One day, while in the bathtub, I noticed several dark patches like scales on a fish all over my butt. When I would rub with a wash cloth, they would fall off very hard to the touch. I went and told my mother. I was taken to a dermatologist, of course. With no sure explanation of why, to no avail, the doctor only gave a diagnosis of some type of allergic reaction to food or bath soap. Oh yes, a prescription for a lotion to apply on my skin for several weeks, which didn't even work.

After eight weeks of oral medications and creams, it seemed to have been a waste of time and money. One thing I did notice, the patches would only appear around the time my monthly periods were to begin. I carried this burden with me wherever I went. I tried to keep not only my feelings hidden but also my body.

Spring of 1967

Love was in the air. I was seventeen years old. I had a crush on my best friend's cousin. After meeting him for the first time, we started dating. *Bam!* I knew I was totally spaced out, head over heels. Little did I know about him. After three months, we got married. Everything happened so fast.

By the fall of 1967, everything began to change. Not only all the leaves on the trees, but also my marriage. My husband and I had to agree to live at his parents' home until the paperwork was completed on our home.

My first day of work at my new job, there I was, my hair standing all over my head, looking like a hot mess. There's no way I could go to work like that. I didn't want to scare the White people. So I got a straightening comb, a chair, and sat in front of the stove in my in-laws' kitchen.

My mother-in-law came down the stairs and asked if she could help. So I agreed. I felt like she should know how to press hair since she had three daughters of her own. It should not be a problem. She made a statement to me, "You sure have a nice grade of hair."

In Black people terms, it means good hair. Oh yeah, whatever. I really didn't pay too much attention until she burnt strands of my hair out three times. All right, that was the last straw. "Just give me the hot comb," I said. "I can finish myself." Truly, I was about to hit the ceiling. Little did I know the nightmare was just about to begin again.

Three weeks had gone by. There I was, standing in front of the bathroom mirror, combing strands of my hair out. In reality, I didn't get too nervous knowing that normally, you could lose about one hundred strands a day.

By the end of the month, my below-the-ear length hair was now about one-fourth inches long. I began looking like a plucked chicken about to be exterminated. I felt the back of my head, reached for a mirror, and I could see three bald spots. I grabbed a scarf, tied it on my head, jumped into the car, and drove to Kansas City, Kansas, to my mother's house to let her see and to get her opinion.

The first words that came out of her mouth were, "What happened to your hair? You have three bald spots about the size of a nickel on the crown of your head." All of sudden, I started screaming from the top of my lungs.

"Go to the doctor," my mother said. "It is possible that it may just be your nerves."

"Oh *God*, I am not nervous nor am I under stress. What am I to do?" I remembered past experiences I had encountered the doctor did not do me any good. So I just continued to pray and sought *God*'s help, went to the nearest wig store, and bought a wig to cover my head and mentally preserve my self-esteem and try not go insane. I remembered the Bible scripture, "Thou wilt keep him in perfect peace, whose mind is stayed on thee; because he trusteth in thee" (Isaiah 26:3 KJV).

One thing for sure, I never forgot all the past experiences I endured. By now, many dreams and visions became a part of me. I didn't quite spiritually understand them all. I never gave up my faith and belief in a higher power, even though several years had gone by, and my hair had never grown back.

　　　　STORMIE CLAY

After five years of marriage, in the spring of 1973, I gave birth to my third child, a boy. During the pregnancy, my calcium levels were below normal. I lost fillings out of my teeth. My dentist advised me to have dental surgery after my baby got older. So I was scheduled to be admitted into a nearby hospital within a week.

During that week, I fell asleep one night. In my dream, I found myself standing in front of the dining room table. There in the middle of the table was one big silver pot, one plate, and one fork. It seemed very weird, for across on the other side of the table stood five of my in-laws, one of which was my mother-in-law. She said, "I cooked a special dish just for you."

I then picked up the plate, then the fork, removed the lid from the pot, and when I looked down into the pot, there were five black snakes crawling around in the bottom. I woke up in my bedroom with cold chills running down my back.

I heard a still small voice say, *Don't eat anything offered to you on a plate or pot.* Once again, *O God, what is going on?* "And it shall come to pass afterward, that I will pour out my spirit upon all flesh; and your sons and daughters shall prophesy, your old men dream dreams, your young men shall see visions" (Joel 2:28 KJV).

From that very moment, I thanked *God* for the warning. I made up excuses for not eating anybody's food. Strange things just kept on occurring. I was removing the linen from off the bed and found a black cord about twelve inches long with knots tied in it. I counted ten in number. The letters in my first and last name. I didn't let on to my husband when he came home that night. I just took the cord, wrapped it in some newspaper, and burned it in the trash.

I never told my husband about the dreams I was having because he wouldn't believe me anyway. I just kept them all to myself and prayed even now more than ever. One thing I do know is that *God* sees everything: the good, the bad, and the ugly.

The day finally came I was admitted into the hospital. The surgery went okay: no complications. While in the recovery room, I was then transferred to another room. While still recovering after sedation, I heard a still voice say, *Your enemies are approaching.*

Okay, Lord Jesus. I lay in bed, didn't move, one eye closed, and the other barely open. My husband and mother-in-law entered the room. I heard them call my name. I just lay there like an old opossum on a dirt road.

The both of them called my name several times. I just moaned as if I was in real bad pain with one eye yet open. That's when I saw my mother-in-law open her purse and take out a medium-sized brown bottle, removed the cap, and poured some type of liquid into my water pitcher, placed the cap back on the bottle, and put it back inside of her purse. Then she said to my husband, "Come on and let's go. She is still under the medication after surgery. She doesn't even know that we are here." They both left the room. I then heard a small still voice say, *Your enemies are now gone.* I got out of the hospital bed, took the water pitcher, and poured the contents into the toilet and flushed.

Summer of 1973 was very hot that year, but my marriage had grown cold. There were now times of physical abuse. I even tried to run away with the children, but my mother would encourage me to go back. Her constant words were, "No man is going to want a woman with children, a ready-made family." So there I was, back in hell again.

Come to think about it, I can't even recall a time when my husband told me he loved me. One night, my husband had supposedly gone to work. The children were all asleep. Then I fell across my bed and drifted off into a deep coma-like sleep. This time, I found myself running away from this giant black snake. You know, this is weird. I had this dream three times before. In fact, during my whole marriage. I made up my mind that I was not going to run anymore but stand and face my enemy. At least that's what the old folks would say, that when you dream of snakes, you had enemies.

So I stopped running and stood still. That's when the snake began to wrap itself around the bottom of my feet, both legs, thighs, until it reached my waist, on up to the middle of my chest. It had a gigantic head, but when I looked into the face of it, the head connected to its body was the head of my husband.

 STORMIE CLAY

I immediately woke up in my bedroom with cold chills and sweat all over. I turned and look at the clock on the nightstand. It was three o'clock in the morning. Once again, my prayer was, "Oh, *God*, help me. What's going on with all the repeated dreams?" I didn't quite understand yet. Deep within, I felt this was some type of spiritual warning. "And he spake a parable unto them to this end, that men ought always to pray and not to faint" (Luke 18:1 KJV).

My husband had a crazy way of showing his love: a couple of slaps upside my head, being accused of having an affair, never a word that he was sorry or forgive me, and he just gave me some money. I got into the car and went to the nearby shopping mall.

After three hours of walking around, my mind was not focused on buying anything but that I was in a marriage with three children and not loved by my husband. I finally walked out the store with a black dress, not even my favorite color, only to take it home and hang it in the closet. Every time I opened the closet door, I stared at that black dress and wondered just when and where I would wear it. Come to think of it, my marriage was becoming just as black and sinister as the dress.

Even when I would lie down and fall asleep, my dreams were turning into nightmares of demons. I now was fighting for my life while awake. Once again, "Oh, *God*, what am I to do now?" The devil was definitely trying to destroy me, and I didn't have anyone to protect me. At least that's what Satan (the devil) wanted me to believe. Again, after laying the children down to sleep, my husband gone, only *God* knows where, I sat down in my favorite chair and fell asleep, only this time, I found myself standing in the middle of the cemetery with three black cars, a group of people, all of whom I didn't recognize, crying.

What stood out in the dream is that there was a bronze casket with a male figure standing at the left end of it, all dressed in a white robe. I proceeded to walk toward the casket to see who was in it. Slowly, as I moved closer, the lid of the casket came open. As I looked down, there was me, dressed in a black dress. Again, I woke up with cold chills.

The next day, at 7:00 a.m., while the children remained asleep, I got up after putting on some clothes. I went into the kitchen to bake a cake for that evening's dinner dessert. While standing at the kitchen counter, the door slowly came open. There, standing in the doorway, was my husband. I spoke to him, but he didn't respond, just staring at me with this dreadful look on his face. "I am not in the mood to argue today."

By that time, he had walked up behind me and placed his arms around my neck and began choking me. I tried to scream out, "You're hurting me."

That's when he said, "I'm trying to kill you."

Really, I don't know what happened next. All I can say is that I found myself walking down this long highway, and at the end of it was a bright light, so bright I could hardly see. Every now and then, there would be a person walking on the left side of the highway, going in the opposite direction. All I wanted to do was reach the light that was before me. When I reached the light, there, standing in front of me, was an individual dressed in a white robe, both sleeves draped at the wrist, arms outstretched. The brightness of light covered his head that I could not see his face.

At that very moment, I began to plead my case. "Lord, don't take me now. Who will take care of my little children? I'm too young to die. I'm only twenty-three years old." I poured out my heart, "Lord, if you would just let me go back and be with them, I would do whatever you wanted me to do." At that very moment, my whole body felt as if someone had poured several buckets of water all over me. Neither my clothes nor the bed linen was wet.

I found myself positioned halfway across the bed. All three of my children were sitting on the floor by the bed, crying. Again I heard a voice say, "Now is the time to get out." I grabbed them up, wrapped a blanket around my seven-month-old baby, called for a cab, and went to my mother's house.

In the meantime, I went to see my doctor. My throat was so sore and painful I couldn't swallow a teaspoon of water. He said there was a possibility that my vocal cords were damaged. My godmother said that I was blessed to be alive. Oh, praise *God* Almighty for His grace

                    STORMIE CLAY

and mercy. "By this I know that thou favourest me, because mine enemy doth not triumph over me" (Psalm 41:11 KJV).

Spring of April 1974, a day before my twenty-fourth birthday, my divorce was final. I received custody of my three children. My mother told me that I couldn't live with her, so my godmother opened the doors of her home to me. I stayed there for six years. I joined her church and gave my life to Jesus Christ. Upon the sudden death of my godmother, I dreaded having to go live with my mother. She criticized me trying to live a saved life and made several derogatory statements about me being a lesbian. I became so fed up I prayed for *God* to help me find my own place to stay. Within two months, I moved out.

Several years of splendid bliss and peace, just me and my children. In the winter of 1984, I met a very decent man about ten years older than me. Again, the devil tried to destroy me. I allowed myself to become spiritually weak, thinking this man and I were going to get married. I found myself pregnant. I gave birth to a baby girl. Even though her dad was nice and took care of her, I asked my younger sister to come over and babysit the other children while I went into the hospital.

She came, but on the second day, I called to check on the children. My mother answered the phone to my surprise. I asked where my younger sister was, and she said that she sent her home. I began to feel uneasy about her being there. I didn't have any choice, so I hung up the phone. The day I was discharged to come home, my mother was not even there to greet me or see her new granddaughter.

Little did I know the evils that I had experienced in the past came back to haunt me. After getting settled back home, I decided to go into my closet and try on my clothes to see what fit.

On removing my clothes from the suitcase and boxes, I noticed that some of them, the buttons were all removed, like cut off with scissors. Pieces had been cut off the blouses. All the baby clothes that I had bought were gone. Then I asked the older children if they saw anything unusual happen while I was gone. Their response was no.

I then called my mother, and her response was a few choice curse words, and she never was going to come back over to my house again. Not to mention that I looked into my refrigerator and shelves to find half of my food was gone. After feeling all disgusted, I went downstairs to wash a few clothes in the basement. The water was coming slowly out of the drain. I looked underneath the stairs at the water meter and pipes, and there was a big pile of dirt. Knowing that there were not any leaks in the basement, I took an old clothes hanger and began to separate the clods of dirt, and to my surprise, there were pieces of my shirts all mixed in.

At that very moment, the phone rang, so I went back upstairs. It was a friend of mine, a woman of *God*. She told me that I was heavy on her heart. I explained to her what I had found. She told me that the dirt had come from the cemetery, and she told me to sweep and dispose of everything under the stairs in the basement. She also said that a person was working against me and that it was an act of witchcraft.

She came over with some of the mothers of her church. They prayed and took bottles of anointing oil and blessed my whole house to rid it of demons. From that very day, I didn't associate with my family. I just continued my life in constant prayer and reading my Bible, going to church as much as possible.

Spring of 2004, I thought life was getting better. Well, spiritually, it was, but past demons began to raise their heads once again. In the month of March, I received a phone call from my mother. It had been several years since I had heard from her. She told me that she was just calling me to let me know that my high school picture that hung on the wall in her bedroom was missing. Someone must have stolen it. I just replied, "Why would someone want to just steal my picture and not take any of the other children's?"

I just hung up the phone and began to pray. I called some of my relatives who had come to visit from out of town and asked them if they removed my picture from off the wall in my mother's bedroom and not tell her. Each one responded with the answer no. There were a couple of times that I went out of town to visit relatives and looked at picture albums and did not see my photo. So I just stored this in the back of my mind, went about my daily activities, working, and taking care of my children.

    STORMIE CLAY

In the year of 2008, the idea of my missing picture resurfaced in my mind over and over to the point I wasn't able to sleep. I told a friend about what had happened, and he told me if I really was concerned about it, if I believed in *God*, then I would just have to pray and ask Him to reveal where my picture was and who had it. So I did. I prayed for three days, and within three days, I went to sleep and had a dream that I was walking inside of a cemetery, and I came to a place in front of an old oak tree with two large tombstones on either side, and as I looked down, I could see someone had freshly dug the dirt from around one of the tombstones. By the way, the cemetery was right across the street from my mother's house.

I now acknowledge that the power of the Holy Spirit has been working all through my life. Again, I heard a still voice say to me that my picture had not been stolen by anyone but had been buried by the tombstones. I woke up early that morning and called my friend and told him about my dream and that I believed *God* had shown me where my picture was. He said that I should go to the cemetery and dig it up. I told him that I didn't want to, I was afraid, and I trusted what I had seen. *God* does not lie. That digging was not necessary.

You know, life is strange sometimes, and we don't know or understand why things happen, why *God* allowed us to go through them. But I can truly say, without a test, there can be no testimony. Nothing in life is over until *God* says it is over. Whatever is done in the dark shall be revealed in the light.

Oh yes, going back in the past, I came home early from school one day, rushed into the bathroom, only to catch my mother off guard behind the door, standing at the sink, holding a pair of scissors and a pair of my panties.

My walk with *God* has given me a heart to forgive my mother, in-laws, and my ex-husband. For the Word of *God* states, "No weapon that is formed against thee shall prosper; and every tongue that shall rise against thee in judgement thou shalt condemn" (Isaiah 54:17 KJV).

Naomi Jones (Stormie Clay) was born in Louisiana and lived most of her life in Kansas. She is a retired nurse and a mother of eight. Naomi Jones (Stormie Clay) has had her poetry recognized by *Who's Who of American Poets*. She is a licensed missionary and dedicated to ministering the Word of God.